Save, Spend, Share

Using Your Money

First American edition published in 2006 by
Compass Point Books
3109 West 50th Street, #115
Minneapolis, MN 55410

Visit Compass Point Books on the Internet at
www.compasspointbooks.com
or email your request to
custserv@compasspointbooks.com

For Compass Point Books
Catherine Neitge, Brandie E. Shoemaker,
Shelly Lyons, Keith Griffin, and Carol Jones

For Allegra Publishing Ltd.
Giles Powell-Smith, Will Webster, Mike Phillips (Beehive Illustration
Agency), Rosie Brooks, Felicia Law, and Karen Foster

Library of Congress Cataloging-in-Publication Data
Bailey, Gerry.
Save, spend, share : using your money / Gerry Bailey & Felicia Law.
p. cm. — (My money)
Includes bibliographical references and index.
ISBN 0-7565-1672-2 (hard cover)
1. Commerce—Juvenile literature. 2. Purchasing—Juvenile literature.
3. Selling—Juvenile literature. 4. Consumption (Economics)—Juvenile
literature. I. Law, Felicia. II. Title. III. Series.
HF353.B34 2006
381—dc22   2005030252

The publishers acknowledge the help of Dr. Joseph Santos, associate professor of
economics, South Dakota State University, and Bob Lovitt and Jo Ruff of Greenaway,
Chartered Accountants, Sevenoaks, Kent, UK, for their consultant input.

Photo credits:
© Kunsthistorisches Museum, Vienna, Austria;
Ali Meyer/Bridgeman Art Library: 8
© Palazzo Ducale, Mantua, Italy / Bridgeman Art Library: 8
© Jon Arnold Images / Alamy: 18

Save, Spend, Share

Using Your Money

by Gerry Bailey & Felicia Law

The spending power of the young people, ages 5-16 years, in the United States is $84 billion and is scheduled to triple by 2007! You make a real difference to the economy of the country. But what are you spending your money on—and why?

COMPASS POINT BOOKS ✦ MINNEAPOLIS, MINNESOTA

In the U.S., advertisers are spending more than $12 billion a year to get you to spend your money on their products!

Table of Contents

Money goes around and around

You pocket the pack of gum and put your coins on the counter. The store clerk places them in the till and half an hour later he hands them out as change. They find themselves in and out of another four tills that same day. At the week's end, they're bagged and delivered to the bank. The bank holds them just two days before they're delivered to an amusement arcade to be given out as change. The change falls into a child's hand. In half an hour it's being handed over the counter of the local candy store in exchange for… and so on. Money goes around and around.

Trade basics

Most of what we do with the money in our pockets involves buying and selling. Even if you don't sell things you make as a business, you will almost certainly be selling your time and effort to earn pocket money or handouts from grateful neighbors or family. You'll know how to get friends to buy your possessions when you've no use for them, including your old bike, your clothes that don't fit any longer, the lipstick you knew wouldn't suit you in the store. And you'll almost certainly know a lot about buying. Like most people your age, you'll have money of your own to spend, and you'll have plenty of ideas about how to spend it.

Buying and selling is all about trade—using our money to buy the things we need and selling to people the things that they need. Trade is what keeps the money moving around. Even people who live a very simple lifestyle will need to trade from time to time, even if they swap one kind of goods for another and don't involve themselves with money at all. They can exchange things they have too much of for things they don't have at all.

Because trade involves an exchange of goods that makes both the seller and the buyer happy, trade always involves an agreement or a deal. You may have to negotiate to get the deal you want—the right price for your bike or the best swap for your lipstick—but the final deal is absolute. You met, you made a deal, you walked away. That's what trade is all about.

A market

- A market describes the act or place of trading.
- A market can be a physical display of goods for sale in the street, but it can also describe a store, a telephone or Web site negotiation—or indeed any act of trade.
- A market prices and sells goods of every kind, from actual things you can pick up to ideas, buildings, even money.
- A market brings buyers and sellers together.

Spend my coin

The word *spend* comes from the Latin word *expendere*, meaning to weigh out. When coins were first minted, they were often handmade and could be uneven in size and weight. Traders would weigh out their gold or silver coins since the value of a coin was in its weight—not in a value stamped on its surface.

Supply and demand

Supply and demand describes the way a market works—how people decide the amount of a product that they are willing to buy. If supply and demand are balanced—the number of people who want to buy matches the number who want to sell—the price will be decided by the market. If any of the costs or benefits change, the demand of buyers will fall. If supplies are limited and difficult to get hold of, the price will go up, and the number of sellers will also change.

How much buyers will purchase of a product depends on their goals:

- tastes
- wants
- needs
- preferences
- the usefulness of the product

When people's goals change, their reasons for buying a product change, too. They may also change the amount of the goods they buy. Of course, your goals will depend on your age, and what you're used to.

A lot of your preferences have to do with where you live. You might buy lots of horse meat steaks if you live in France, for example—but you probably won't buy any if you don't!

Price

Price is also important. People have a limited amount of money to spend, and if they spend more on one thing, they cannot spend it on another. When the price of a product goes up, other competitive and cheaper products will sell better. People will buy more hamburger if the price is $2 per pound than if it is $4.

Income

The amount of income people earn helps decide how much they buy. If a person with a low income spends $1,000 on a trip around the world, he or she will have to cut back on buying food, clothing, or shelter. If a wealthy person makes the same investment, he or she may not need to cut other spending at all.

When people earn more, they spend more—mostly on what are called normal goods, things like food, vacations, and entertainment. They also cut back on what are called inferior goods. Public transportation is an example— people stop taking the bus and start to drive their own cars.

Fashion

Denim jeans are a good example of how fashion and taste affect people's spending. People with higher incomes didn't buy jeans when they first appeared, because they were considered to be working-class clothes. But when they were adopted by youth in the 1950s and 1960s, they moved into high fashion.

Product switch

Some products sell well one moment and not the next. This is usually because buyers have switched to another product. They may switch back again at any moment. These kinds of products are known as substitute products. For example, if beef prices are high, people may be tempted to stop eating beef and buy chicken instead. Another reason is fashion. If chicken burgers are in, then hamburgers may well be less popular and demand will fall.

There are some products that are always safe. These are like parasites—they cling to the back of other popular goods. For example, if hamburgers are selling well, ketchup will sell well, too. Ketchup is known as a complementary product.

Sometimes goods are such good complements that they're sold together and we think of them as a single item. Left shoes and right shoes are an example!

Isabella
art shopper extraordinaire

Isabella, Marquess of Mantua, was born in Ferrara, Italy, in 1474. She was the daughter of Duke Ercole I of Ferrara and Eleonora of Aragon. After a very cultured education, she was married at the age of 16 to the wealthy Francesco Gonzaga.

Isabella enjoyed art, music, and poetry and was one of the most outstanding and refined women of the Renaissance period.

She was disappointed to find that her new home in the Gonzaga palace was a little drab and set about buying art treasures to decorate it.

On her shopping trips, Isabella would travel hundreds of miles by barge along the river Po to the port of Venice. Here she would meet the trading ships arriving with treasures from the East: porcelain, carvings, sculptures, gold, and precious jewels. Isabella would pile the barge high and sail back to Mantua.

Eventually she made Mantua into one of the top cultural centers of Europe. Fascinated by beautiful things and antiques, she enriched the rooms of the palace and especially her studio and the two small bridal chambers—Camere degli Sposi—given to her by her husband. Here Isabella gathered all kinds of masterpieces: small bronzes, rare manuscripts, musical instruments, and a globe on which she followed Columbus' voyages.

She also commissioned painters to decorate the art-filled apartments with frescoes that still can be seen today. The most famous of these is by Andrea Mantegna on the walls of the Camere degli Sposi. This masterpiece took the artist nine years to complete. In it, he included paintings of many of the rich and foreign visitors to the court and late 15th century court life.

Trading since time began

Trading has been going on since time began. From the point where early man settled in one place and grew crops, he often found he had too much of the things he'd grown and too little of the things he hadn't. So, he was up for swaps! He needed to exchange his surplus goods for something he didn't have but needed. And this meant going to market and making a trade.

The earliest trade was just this—swapping one set of goods for another. Of course, both buyer and seller had to agree on a value for their goods—and both had to want what the other one had—which wasn't always easy. Eventually, money in the form of coins, and later notes, was introduced as the medium of exchange. This meant that money became an accepted alternative to goods and had a value of its own. In other words, goods could now be swapped or traded for money.

Just a few centuries later, trade was opening up the world. It wasn't just a case of going to a neighbor's field or to the nearest market for what you wanted. Now traders crossed oceans and continents and established trade routes that crisscrossed the globe.

Great traders

It's easy to take for granted the silk clothes we buy from China and Thailand, the tea we drink from India, the grapes flown in from South America, or the car your mom's just bought from Japan. International trade is the name of the game today. But 700 years ago, all of this was just building.

In the late 1200s, Marco Polo left Venice with his father and uncle to travel due east toward China and the cities of the great Kublai Khan. He retraced his steps years later along the newly established trading route known as the Silk Road.

Later, sea explorers like Columbus, Vasco da Gama, and Magellan set off in ships with the most basic of charts and maps and nautical equipment. They hoped to discover new rich countries where they could gather up exotic local products—from tobacco and spices to gold.

Throughout the 1500s and 1600s, the world of trade opened up overland and across oceans, with great ports opening as bustling merchant centers and rich people bought goods they'd never seen before.

Marrakech

Marrakech is one of the great markets of the world. For centuries it offered a rich oasis on the edge of the Sahara and was a stopping station for the great trading caravans that traveled between Africa and Europe. It served as a place to buy and sell goods ranging from magic potions to magic carpets.

The heart of Marrakech is Jemaa el Fna, a huge open square where today, performers gather in the late afternoon and evening. For a few *dirhams*—the local coin — you can watch snake charmers, acrobats and tumblers, water sellers with their chests covered in dangling brass cups, and sit on the ground to listen to the storytellers.

The souk in Luxor, Egypt

The longest souk

The Aleppo souk stretches for about 20 miles (32 km) and is covered by stone archways. This makes it the longest covered souk in the Middle East, and it is one of the best. Once the most important trade area in Syria, it is still an important shopping area, where the past meets the present. Souks are found in many of

The Souk

Morocco's cities. A souk is the commercial quarter of an Arab city, but the term has come to describe the huge covered markets made up of hundreds of narrow passageways, packed with small shops and stalls. The narrow, winding streets and alleys of the souk are far more orderly than they first appear. One street will sell only leather slippers. The next few sell only brass kettles and then a whole section of crisscrossing alleys is given over to lamps and nothing else. These specialty "souks within a souk" are devoted to fabrics, spices, brass and ironwork, clothing, and other wares.

Haggling

Haggling is the name of the game. When presented with a price, counter with a price of about one third the amount. Keep the process friendly yet firm. If you counter with a final offer and are allowed to walk away without buying, you've obviously underestimated the value.

Here, too, is the daily market for meat and vegetables. The meat souk, with its open-air displays of goats' heads, sheep's feet, and live chickens, is best experienced in the morning hours, before the heat of day turns the hot air smelly and foul. The form of negotiation used in the souk is known as haggling. Goods are often examined and haggled for over glass after glass of the national drink—hot, sweet, mint tea.

Markets

If you have something to sell and you need to find someone to buy it, the only missing piece of the puzzle is the place. Where do seller and buyer come together to make the exchange? Traditionally, a deal could easily be made in the open street, but if sellers wanted to get the best price and buyers wanted to compare a range of goods, it was best to attend a marketplace—a gathering of people sharing a common goal—to trade.

What can I get you to drink?

Half an O-positive please

Open market

Open markets started almost 1,000 years ago and are the earliest known trading places. In many countries, markets were first held in small towns where the lord who owned the land would establish a market along with a fair to increase his income. This income was made by charging tolls and fines on all those who came to trade.

A huge marketplace would be laid out, marked by a stone cross and sometimes by public scales. It was big enough for sheep and cattle pens and all kinds of stalls and sideshows. Sales of livestock and local produce, leather goods from the local tannery, wool from the shearers, woven baskets, and copperware would be carried on.

Fairs were even bigger trading occasions than markets, and not held just for amusement. Sometimes they lasted for days. Other fairs were added in later centuries and traders, including merchants buying wool, were attracted to the market from far and wide. At fairs called "mops," large numbers of domestic servants would attend looking for jobs.

Today, daily, weekly, or monthly street markets are still colorful affairs, popular for their cheap, fresh produce. They vary widely around the world and by season, since they reflect local conditions. You will find many kinds of chili peppers in Mexico, piles of kava roots in Fiji, durians in Southeast Asia, dates in North Africa, live snakes in Hong Kong, and seasonal fruits and flowers everywhere.

There are famous markets in many cities, including the French Market in New Orleans, Covent Garden in London, and Les Halles in Paris. Middle Eastern cities such as Marrakech and Aleppo have famous souks. New York and Los Angeles have teeming garment districts where clothing is designed, manufactured, and sold.

Flea market

The term *flea market* comes from the translation of the French *Marché aux Puces*, an open-air street market for inexpensive or secondhand articles that operated in Paris around the 1920s. It literally translates to "market with fleas."

Famous flea markets exist in many cities. Portabello Market in London becomes a street market for antiques once a week. The San Jose Flea Market in California is one of the world's largest. It offers food, live music, entertainment, and more than 2,000 booths with arts and crafts, antiques, comics, jewelry, furniture, and much more.

Pricing

A rule on market prices: a seller can always go down on a price, but they can never go back up. If you're selling, price items about a third of what they would cost new. Clothes are generally very poor sellers so price them cheap. Some buyers will expect to bargain with you.

The specific

Many shops still believe in carving out a niche for themselves as a boutique—a shop that specializes in a certain product rather than selling a variety of items. Young people spend a great deal of money on athletic shoes, for example, so a number of stores have opened up that sell only these. Boutiques may specialize in ties, underwear, or even pens. They can be an Aladdin's cave of interesting bits and pieces and are usually staffed by equally dedicated and interesting people. They usually offer a wider range of their particular product than the general stores. They offer a one-stop trip for people who know exactly what they want.

The general

Do you expect to buy goldfish food in the grocery store? A hair band in the newspaper shop? A newspaper at the garage? Seems odd but it's what happens. More and more, stores narrow down their stock to the most frequently requested items and only put them on display. A single store can sell a whole range of items. Some are old-fashioned "corner shops" that stock everything the local community could possible need—until the space runs out. Some, like gas stations, exploit the fact that once you've stopped your car and got out of it, you're fair game!

Convenience shopping, as it's called, is the new trend, because people work longer and longer hours and have little time to shop from store to store. So whether you're a local or a stranger in town, convenience stores always look and feel the same and carry much the same stock—so no confusion!

Did you know?

The largest fashion retail chain in America is Gap. It was developed in 1969 by American Don Fisher and his wife, Doris. This was after Don lost his temper when he tried to exchange a pair of jeans he'd bought from a local store with little success. The first shop was called Gap to highlight the fact that young people seemed to be getting a raw deal from the retailers—who were often older people. In other words the generation "gap" seemed to be working against young people. Today there are Gap stores all over the world.

Top brands

Companies get very excited about brands these days. They don't look at things as just products. So what is a brand? Well, a brand can be a product, a group of products, or a company. But it's more than that. It's a name and an association. It's what sticks in your mind when you think of a product or group of products. They are usually valuable

assets because people are willing to pay more for products from a company with a strong brand.

Coca-Cola is probably the brand people around the world recognize most. It means that when you think of a brown, sweet, fizzy drink that makes you feel good, the first words that come into your mind are Coca-Cola. Nike is

another brand name that is instantly recognizable. But a brand is also a promise. Almost every owner of a famous brand has tried hard to establish a

set of values that consumers will like and understand. Owners want their brand to represent something trustworthy and honest. Each year people are questioned about what they think are the best brands. Can you match the logos shown here to these brand names?
Gap • Disney • Coca-Cola
McDonald's • Nike
Tommy Hilfiger • KFC

The largest shopping center in the world is in Edmonton, Alberta, with 800 stores

Auctions

Not everything has a price tag on it. The price of an object is set by supply and demand—if no one wants it, it will sell very cheaply. If everyone wants it, the price can go through the roof. Auctions are an interesting way to get to a final price based on supply and demand. Of course, if you know your antiques or vintage car market—or exactly who painted what picture and when—you'll be able to accurately judge the price of something. But there are many objects that come up for auction where the price is entirely set by you and your fellow buyers.

Talk the Biz!

Reserve price
This is the minimum price that the seller is prepared to sell at. An item that doesn't achieve a high enough bid will be taken out of the sale.

Bidding war
When two bidders start competing to buy an item, they push the price up and up in what's called a bidding war.

Inspection

Customers gather before the auction starts. This is when objects are inspected, picked up, and examined for names, dates, and tiny flaws. This is when a chip on an antique vase drops its value by hundreds. Most auctioneers print a catalog or list of all items up for sale. You should mark your catalog to highlight any items you're interested in and pencil in your estimated price.

Valuation

As we have said, the value of anything is the value someone is prepared to pay for it. But most items have a market value, too. This is based on what people have generally been prepared to pay for a similar item.

Professional dealers will have valued the goods, too. The auctioneer may already have phoned them with information on the best items, and anything of real value will be given a reserve price.

Your valuation is likely to be based on how much you want the object and how much money you're prepared to spend. But it may be influenced by the market value, too. Many items bought at auction are purchased as investments. They are prized objects that will go up and up in value.

Bidding

A bid is an offer of money. The auctioneer invites everyone to open the bids for an item as each comes up for sale. The bidding doesn't start at zero. It starts close to the market valuation or the reserve price that's already been placed on the item. You may hear bidding starting at $1,000; other times the auctioneer might ask for someone in the room to start the bid at $1. This could be you!

You have to stay alert. Once the auction starts, the bids come fast and furious. As each buyer signals to the auctioneer, the price starts to rise. It might go up gently, $1 at a time, but it's unlikely. What usually happens is that the bidding goes up in $10 jumps or $100 jumps—so you must stay awake. You need to know where the price has risen to before you start waving at the auctioneer. And be careful! There are stories of people scratching their ear, only to find they've bought something for $1 million!

The day they sold New York

One of America's most famous land deals took place in 1626 when the Dutch bought Manhattan. Peter Minuit, representing the Dutch West India Company, paid 60 guilders (the equivalent of about $24) for Manhattan Island. It's now worth more than $60 billion!

Minuit paid the Canarsie Indians, who didn't own the island in the first place. It was owned by the Wappingers, but they didn't object to the sale. A letter sent back to the Netherlands documents the sale, stating "... the island Manhattes was bought from the wildmen, for the worth of 60 guilders." The Dutch colony was first called New Amsterdam and then renamed New York after the English took it over.

Going for a song

When we say something is "going for a song" today, we mean something is selling cheap, or for less than it's worth. But that's not how the phrase started out.

In fact, the "song" that the phrase describes was not a song at all, but a poem: *The Faerie Queen* was presented to Queen Elizabeth I of England by its author, Edmund Spencer. It was his most popular poem, but Lord Burleigh, the Lord High Treasurer didn't think so.

When he heard that the queen was going to pay Spencer for the poem, he famously said, "What! All this for a song?" But the queen insisted on making the payment to Spencer.

The incident was reported everywhere, and the phrase became part of English slang. However, it came to mean low payment rather than high because of the small change that was tossed to entertainers and singers around London.

Stake your claim

You see something you want, but you can't afford to buy it. What you might be able to do, though, is "stake your claim" to it by putting down a deposit that will ensure that no one else will buy it until you pay in full.

The phrase "stake your claim" is connected to the gold rushes in California and Alaska. Miners staked their claims in order to mine the gold on a particular piece of ground.

Each claim was a piece of land some no more than 100 square feet (9 square meters) in size. It was either staked out with poles driven into the ground, or marked by a name board erected in the middle of the claim. Then the miners would leave a shovel or pick stuck in the ground as a sign that the claim was still active.

Only when the claim was fully registered with a document did the miner have rightful ownership to all minerals found on it.

Top shops

Shops have come a long way since the earliest days when peddlers walked the streets of cities and country roads, selling their wares from a small horse and cart or even a simple tray. And even when shops started to open in the main street, they would be pretty limited— a butcher, a baker, and a candlestick maker, or, more likely, a hardware store, a haberdasher, a leather worker making shoes and bags, and a tailor making clothes for the rich. Your grandparents will remember a time when there were no music stores selling CDs, and certainly no stores selling MP3 players and TVs. It may sound like the Dark Ages, but the whole tradition of the store as we know it today is relatively new.

Talk the Biz!

Haberdasher

The word *haberdasher* comes from the old Anglo-French word for a type of fabric called *hapertas*. In Great Britain and Australia it means a dealer in dressmaking and sewing goods, such as buttons, needles, ribbons, and thread. In North America it's a dealer in men's clothing. When it appeared in the 1400s it meant a trader in a range of goods, from glasses and swords to bird cages and books.

Young Charles Lewis Tiffany began work in his father's cotton mill, but he soon branched out on his own, establishing a fancy goods and stationary store. He sold a variety of items including Chinese curiosities. Then, in 1847, he began to sell gold jewelry.

A year later his luck escalated. Because of a series of "disturbances" in Europe, the price of diamonds in Paris dropped by 50 percent. Tiffany took advantage of this and made a large purchase. Things were taking off. During the American Civil War he even made swords for soldiers. At the Paris Exhibition in 1867 he was honored for his silver designs, the first American company to win the European prize. The name Tiffany and Company has since been linked with diamonds and fine jewelry.

The English love having tea in the afternoon—a sedate affair with wafer-thin cucumber sandwiches, small cream cakes, and a cup of Indian or Ceylon tea. The tradition has being going on for centuries, and Fortnum and Mason, a famous store in the heart of London, still carries it on. The store is really a great grocery shop, particularly famous as the supplier of food to the Queen of England.

The shop was started in the early 1700s by a servant to Queen Anne of England. As a footman in the royal palace, one of William Fortnum's duties was to light the royal candles. Each day, the half-burned ones had to be replaced with new ones. William took the old stubs and sold them to the ladies at the court. Joined by his landlord, Hugh Mason, their candle trade soon flourished and became an elite supplier of foods.

You didn't have to visit the store in those days. During the war with Napoleon, wealthy army officers would have their Fortnum and Mason box or hamper sent to France so they could still enjoy favorite foods.

Charles Henry Harrod was already a successful wholesaler and tea merchant when he took over a small Knightsbridge shop in 1849. Trade was prosperous, however, and under his son the business grew. It was due, they said, to hard work and careful planning. The Knightsbridge district itself must have helped, though, providing a wealthy clientele.

In 1889 Harrods became a public limited company and under its managing director, Richard Burbridge, it grew in leaps and bounds. In 1902 it was London's largest store, offering quality and service to anyone. It boasted 91 departments and needed more than 2,000 staffers. Its motto was "Everything for Everybody Everywhere."

Today it is still a famous landmark and visited by customers from all over the world.

The Old Curiosity Shop

A tale written by the famous English writer, Charles Dickens.

Each evening, Master Humphrey took a walk though the city of London gathering information on the characters and businesses he came across. One night he was approached by a sweet, pretty little girl who asked him to help her find her way home because she was lost. Humphrey agreed and finally arrived at a doorway, where an old graying man, her grandfather, let them in.

Master Humphrey learned that the grandfather loved the child, Little Nell, so much that he would do anything to make her happy. They lived together in an old curiosity shop full of old items.

"There were suits of mail standing like ghosts in armor here and there, fantastic carvings brought from monkish cloisters, rusty weapons of various kinds, distorted figures in china and wood and iron and ivory: tapestry and strange furniture that might have been designed in dreams."

Master Humphrey also learned that Little Nell's grandfather was in debt to the horrible Mr. Quilp, his employer. Quilp and his fellow villains were so greedy that they had no sense of morality. Quilp even eyed Little Nell as a potential wife should his first wife die.

Finally, Nell and her grandfather

were forced to flee from the grip of Quilp. They drifted through cities of industrial England pursued by Quilp, finally settling in a pretty country hamlet. But Little Nell was now ill and she died. Her grandfather followed soon after. Their innocence and goodness had been destroyed.

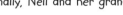

Shop design

Which are your favorite stores? You'll certainly have some. Everyone does! It's one of the things about consumers that retailers rely on. One of the most surprising things about our shopping habits is that we tend to visit a few favorite stores over and over again and rarely change our shopping pattern. We know the stores that suit us! We like the way they're laid out, the goods they carry, the staff perhaps. We like the fact that when we visit them, everything is exactly as we would expect to find it. There are no surprises. We feel comfortable. But don't be fooled. To the store planners we're traffic, people whose shopping habits have been well analyzed and are well understood!

Atmosphere

The layout of stores varies enormously, from the shop piled high with boxes and goods, to the serene minimalism of a cell phone shop with lots of low lighting and shiny steel. Whatever the decor, it will have been planned with one thing in mind—to create the best atmosphere to make you buy. Retailers know all about atmosphere.

If a store sells lots of lines at inexpensive prices, it will have a more crowded feel—racks and racks of clothing, stacks and stacks of sweaters, all with bold price tickets. The aisles will be narrow so you're packed together with other

shoppers, so you feel part of the crowd and are surrounded on all sides by lots of lovely, exciting things. Hot music and busy clerks will add to the atmosphere.

If the store is selling a lifestyle product, it may have wider, more spacious aisles, cool colors, just a few carefully chosen items placed at eye level—even a seat or two and soft music playing. The products may be expensive, but the layout makes you feel sophisticated and expensive, too. So, once again, you feel comfortable.

Loyalty

Amazingly, we each have just a few favorite stores where we buy everything we need. In fact, we have a shopping beat. We tread the same route down the street, passing some stores and entering others. We position ourselves—knowing where and what we need to buy. Even the razzmatazz of a new store opening rarely changes our pattern. We know what we like!

And the stores know this. They do everything they can to make us feel like old friends when we walk in, and they also make sure we feel comfortable once we're there. Singapore Airlines, for instance, makes sure its business passengers are all called by name from the moment they step on board. Wouldn't that be nice! A store that greeted you on the loud speaker as you came through the doors—"Why hello Elizabeth! Welcome back!"

Loyalty is valuable. A store may offer you a store card—their own credit card with enticing discounts—when you buy there. They know credit cards bring customers back. At the same time, the store knows why you shop there—it won't be changing the layout too often or even changing the window style.

They want to stay on your beat!

Shoplifting

Goods may be laid out to grab the shopper's attention, but they also attract the attention of shoplifters. The majority of shoplifters are not professionals. Shoplifters of all ages contribute to the $10 billion losses reported by stores in the United States. The losses are not forgotten. Honest consumers pay a lot more for their goods to cover these thefts. And thousands of people end up with a police record.

POP!

Pop is shoptalk for the point of purchase, sometimes called the point of sale—the place where you meet the product! In a store this is the rack or shelf where the product is laid out.

But is it all laid out at random on the off-chance that you might stop and pick it up? Probably not! The shopkeeper knows that up to three-quarters of all purchases are made by customers who are sauntering aimlessly around the store. They will buy on impulse. But they also spend only 10 seconds looking at any one rack or shelf. So the goods must all be displayed at the right level—within eyeshot and easy reach. They must be packaged to catch your eye. But there must be entertainment, too. Free-standing displays mean you have to walk around or behind the product, perhaps look up or peek under. It's a game of hide-and-seek designed to keep you interested, to keep you guessing. You're not just spending money—you're having fun!

Skinny and dizzy

The average size of a woman in the United States is size 14. The average size of a mannequin showing the clothes in the window is size 6! Why? Because clothes look better when they're pinched around a bony figure with no bottom? Who knows? Advertisers pitch the idea that bumpy and lumpy is less attractive—and skinny is best. And there are plenty of magazines, TV programs, and advertisements out there to remind us—just in case we forget.

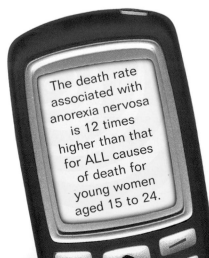
The death rate associated with anorexia nervosa is 12 times higher than that for ALL causes of death for young women aged 15 to 24.

Our preoccupation with being skinny has reached ridiculous proportions, affecting young people's health and rational thinking. Twenty percent of young people suffering from anorexia will die prematurely from complications related to their eating disorder.

Dressing the window

Do you have a really good eye for detail, proportion, and color, and do you possess a vast imagination? Are you creative and practical? If so, you could be the perfect window designer, dressing store window displays, exhibitions in museums, or international shows, as well as many other establishments. Window dressing sets out to display goods to their best advantage. Clothes are draped on elegant plastic models. "You too could look as elegant as this," the windows shout. Other goods are displayed in exciting piles that glitter and glow to catch the eye. "This would look just as good in your home," they say.

Just think of the major store windows and displays at festive times and you'll see that display artists can create fantasy worlds in relatively small spaces. Of course, window dressers have everything in the store to help them create this sense of theater using lighting, costumes, dummies, even intricate electrically operated robots, moving tracks, bobbing heads, and animated puppets.

Bargain hunting

We all love a bargain. Nothing feels quite as good as buying something "on the cheap." You get exactly what you wanted and you've still got cash to spare. Finding a bargain isn't difficult, particularly today when cheap products are flooding the market from abroad. We're all getting into the habit of expecting to pay less rather than more, hunting from store to store for that item that's a bit cheaper and looking for the marked down or special offer item. There are plenty of places to find them!

Street vendors

Street vendors stand on city street corners and appear to be selling the very same things as the stores in the street—except they're far, far cheaper. It all looks like a great bargain. But remember that if you want to return the product for any reason, the street vendor may not be there the next day, while the store certainly will. Apart from this risk, street vendors offer good deals and often get their hands on clearance stock—huge amounts of last season's fashions, stock from a company that has closed down and sold everything off for a song, even stuff rescued from fire or flood disasters.

However, be aware of the few dishonest street vendors, where your risk is far greater. Look closely at goods that have well-known brand names but sell at ridiculous prices. These goods

may be counterfeit. A single letter in the brand name may have been changed to avoid problems with the law but to make you think it's OK. Of course, you might think it's cute or clever to buy one, but in many countries this is an illegal product. They may even be stolen goods, such as cameras, jewelry, or watches. Be aware of these scams, and make sure you know where your money is going, for what, and to whom!

Outlet stores

Outlet stores are a fairly recent arrival on the bargain shopping scene. Designers and manufacturers of every kind of product change their designs and stock each year— sometimes more than once. The old stuff must go to make way for the new. Outlet stores often specialize in designer labels and seasonal fashions, so even if you're one season behind, you can still wear that cool label!

Bankrupt stock

You may see sale signs advertising bankrupt stock of bikes, cameras, or TVs. These are often genuine sales arising from the closure of a company. There will be good bargains to pick up, but remember to check that you still get a warranty in case things go wrong. And make sure you invest in some extra spare parts if they're available, since the manufacturer won't be there to replace breakages in the future.

Charity shops

Charity shops are full of bargains. They only sell the best of the stuff given to them, and you may find designer label clothes, handbags, and other items hidden among the stock. This is the perfect place to set yourself up when you leave home—sheets, saucepans, rugs— it's all likely to be there. And you are doing some good when you buy. Every charity shop is run to raise funds for a cause, and you're helping them in their efforts with every small purchase.

Home shopping

Mail order

Buying the mail order way should be cheaper. After all, there are no store costs to add to the price of goods, no big buildings to carpet and keep clean, no salespeople, store detectives, or window-dressers to train and employ. Of course, you miss out on the hustle and bustle of shopping, but even if mail order buying is a bit short on excitement, there's still all the thrill of receiving your packages, trying things on, and, in many cases, the benefit of paying later.

Ads for all kinds of goods run in newspapers, magazines, and in the large mail order catalogs that weigh as much as a telephone directory. The biggest problems are that photos generally make things look better than they are. Well, that's the photographer's job!

However, you do have the option to return what you don't want—the mail order companies are hoping you won't—or to re-order in a different color or size. Remember to unwrap all products carefully—you'll need to repackage them exactly as they came if you want your refund in full. And always keep a record of what you return.

On the Web

Online marketing people are focusing more and more on the youth market, and young people are buying more and more on the Web. Because buying online is so easy, there has to be a downside to it, and there is.

Compulsive buying happens when you feel a need to buy—whether you have the money to do it or not. Compulsive buyers, like compulsive gamblers, can't help themselves. If you feel that you're getting even close to this state, get help!

TV shopping

There are more and more shopping channels appearing on TV. It's become a huge business—and extremely popular. You may think shopping off a screen is for older folks, or people who work from home all day and who have nothing better to do than browse the shopping channels.

You're probably not even remotely interested in gadgets that slice cucumbers, earrings with 10 carat diamonds, or exercise machines for reducing your hips. But some of the jewelry is quite unique and some of the makeup offers may appeal. Then again, you might find yourself sick and confined to bed for a week or two—with nowhere to shop! Avoid the countdown auctions where you're encouraged to place your order before the stock sells out. This is a ruse to make you think you're playing a clever game. And always compare prices. Goods sold on TV are often more pricey than the same products sold in stores.

Direct mail

Direct mail selling usually starts with an introductory letter and offers you some sort of add-on gift that will be added to your purchase. This is the bait. Check exactly what you're buying and what you're getting free, but if you like receiving mail and getting offers, this can be an interesting way to shop for collectable items—books, magazines, or music.

Telemarketing

Some companies try to get your attention by calling you at home. There are restrictions, however, on who can call. And however good the product, however polite the caller, this is not so successful as companies that advertise their products and ask you to call them free of charge so they can tell you more.

NEVER send cash though the mail! Use a check or money order and keep a record of every payment.

Advertising

Manufacturers who make products need to advertise. If no one knows about their product, they're unlikely to make any sales. So advertising is all about informing consumers about products. Or is it? Advertising is also about persuading you to buy.

It's about making you think you need something when maybe you don't. This means using techniques that are less about information and more about selling a message, conveying a dream, or being downright misleading—even dishonest.

Fast-food retailers have long since given up on the plain hamburger! Now it's bigger and taller than ever!

Sell theory

Advertising is a subtle business. Advertisers don't stand up and say "We want to convince you in any way we can that you must own our product." They use far more clever techniques, and almost all ads are based on one or another of them.

There's the ad that tells you everyone else is buying the product, so if you don't, you're going to feel left out, not "part of the crowd." This is a way of making you feel that everyone else is right or knows something you don't. It's a powerful message because we all enjoy fitting in with our friends, but it shouldn't be the reason we buy. Another similar approach is to use a celebrity you admire to sell the product. After all, if someone famous uses it, you might have a chance of fame yourself. Just remember that these celebrities have been paid a chunk of money to appear in the ad.

Another technique is to play on your emotions—to sell you a dream. Just by owning this product, you will become muscular, beautiful, a sure winner. The music lulls you into a happy or excited mood. The scenery changes from the beach to a private yacht to a Ferrari spinning along the coast. A persuasive voice tells you all this might be yours. It all sounds and looks very tempting. Remember, you live in the real world even if the ad doesn't.

Pulling a fast one

The worst kind of ad is downright misleading. An actor dressed as a doctor tells you that the best kind of fitness comes from running, then points to a running machine with a big brand name on it. It looks as if the machine has sound medical backing, as if doctors everywhere believe it's good for you. Other misleading ads tell you that a product is far better than its competitors. But there's no hard evidence offered to prove it.

Be aware of these techniques. They're all there to make you buy—not because anyone is thinking of your happiness! Use your own judgment.

Market research

Long before an advertisement is launched to the public, the manufacturers and advertisers have spent time and money trying to find out who will buy and why.

This is called market research. Researchers will decide what age group, what income group, and what geographical group at which to aim their product. You wouldn't, for instance, want to aim your newest ice-making machine at reindeer herders in frozen Lapland. But you might aim a new, inexpensive basketball shoe at young people who don't have much money to spend.

Talk the Biz!

Consumer
A person who buys products on a regular basis and whose buying habits can be predicted.

Target market
A particular group or section of the population whose buying habits fit a certain pattern.

Target market!

As we've seen, young people between the ages of 9 and 14 spend millions each year. The outcome of this tremendous buying power is that they're the prime target of advertisers. Because of their youth, they're expected to be less savvy, easier to persuade, easier to influence. Magazines aimed at the younger market are packed with ads for clothing, skin products, entertainment hardware, CDs, and movies. Television ads target the times when you're most likely to be watching to sell you fast foods and sports equipment. Hollywood produces movies by the dozens that are focused on your needs and interests. In the stores, cheaper copies of high-fashion clothes fill rack upon rack in every style and color. It's difficult to resist!

Rent this space

In 1984, a Canadian farmer began renting advertising space on his cows.

Savvy consumer

Research shows that the younger you are, the more likely you will be to believe that an advertising message is truthful, accurate, and unbiased. In the United States, advertisers are spending more than $12 billion a year to target your pocket, and you're watching more than 40,000 of their advertisements a year. That's a lot of pressure!

What's more, the research also shows that young people DO typically respond well to advertising and do go out and buy. You remember the ads better than grown-ups, and you form preferences from the screen long before you buy the product and decide that you do or don't like it.

Why aren't you worried? The last thing you want to be is a pawn in someone else's plans. You don't want to feel manipulated. And you certainly don't want to be influenced by grown-up ads that are shown when you are watching TV and that suggest that drinking beer, using slimming foods, or eating fast food is a great way to spend your life.

It's time to get savvy and start using your spending power. Recognize advertising for what it is. Use your own judgment. Make your own choices. This is your money and your life and if you're to manage both as YOU want, then make sure you stay in charge.

Spending power

Statisticians are watching you all the time—recording how much you're spending and where. This is because you spend so much! The spending power of the 9 million young people, ages 5-16 years, in the United States is predicted to reach $243 billion by 2007!

You can see that you make a real difference to the economy, so the retailers who sell you things and the manufacturers who make it for you want to know all about you. Everyone is trying to predict what you will buy, what's "in" and what's "out," which is your favorite store or brand, and what trends are coming up. You are BIG BUSINESS!

People who collect information about your spending power and your buying habits mostly work for market research companies, but educators, statisticians, and governments do, too. Data like this is known as demographics.

Spending power

Tweens
The many million strong group known as "tweens" (ages 8 to 12) have more spending power than ever before.
• The average allowance is $9 per week.

• Tweens want to feel and look older, like their older siblings, and their taste is for more grown-up products.
• They love cell phones.

Teens
Teenagers from 13 to 15 years old are particularly savvy. They receive and spend more in an attempt to gain privacy, freedom from parents, and from rules and routine. Life is focused on fun, fashion, and friends.

Pester power
Young people exercise enormous control over family spending through "pester power," the power to persuade parents to spend money.

• Children start early—from 3 years old—and by the time they're 10, they are experts at pester power.
• Seventy percent of young people say they influence what parents buy for them.

Best buys
• Two-thirds of your money is spent on sweets and chocolates.
• Girls spend the rest on clothes, shoes, magazines, and makeup.
• Boys spend the rest on more food and drink, computer games, videos, and CDs.

Cell phones
Cell phones are a popular way to keep in touch with friends, play games, and display the latest fashion accessory.

• The world now has more than 1 billion mobile phones.
• More than half of U.S. teens use cell phones.
• The average age for getting a cell phone is 14 years old.

TRU trends

What will the latest Personal Carrying Device, sorry—bag—look like? What will the new trend be? Trends in fashion, sports, cars, or any other item can be followed or they can be created. Manufacturers like to keep an eye on trends so that they can create goods that will fit into them. They may even use a company like Teen Research Unlimited to help them. TRU monitors trends among teens and predicts future ones—even employing a Coolest Brand meter. Clever manufacturers will spot a trend right at the beginning and jump on the bandwagon right away.

So what's next? A bubble gum booster that replaces flavor in worn-out gum. Or shoe gear that helps you run home after school? Any ideas? Manufacturers worldwide are waiting to hear from you!

A bubble gum booster for used and tasteless gum

Advertising

Advertisers think you're fickle. They think you show no loyalty to any brand and will shift your spending power to whatever is cool or most fashionable at the time. Does that sound like you?
• The average young person will have received 250,000 media messages involving lots of advertising by the time they're 15.

So they may think you're fickle, but they know how to reach you. And of course, they're hoping that as you grow up, you'll start being loyal to certain brands—theirs!

Personal care

• There are 25 million young people in the United States, each spending about $4 a week on personal care products—that's a whopping $9.5 billion annually.
• The manufacturers are using young models, movie and pop stars, mall events, and cell-phone marketing to reach them.

You spend

Check out the things you most like to spend money on:

• movie/concert trips
• clothes
• candy and snacks
• shoes
• computer games
• sporting events
• books
• cell phones
• magazines
• cosmetics and toiletries
• CDs, videos
• other

Are you budgeting for all of this? You see some expensive athletic shoes. Do you:
• save until you can buy them?
• earn money from chores?
• pester your parents for the extra cash?
• ask for them as an advance birthday gift?

Anything to learn from your answers?

All about shopping

There is no doubt that most people enjoy shopping. Just planning a shopping trip can be exciting enough—where to go, what to look at, what to try on, and possibly buy. And coming home with loads of shopping bags is a bonus. We all enjoy the thrill of spending our money when the choice is so wide, and when owning new and trendy things makes us feel really good about ourselves. We'd all agree that shopping can lift our spirits. So what's wrong with a bit of "retail therapy?"

Needs versus wants

It doesn't take a genius to tell you what's wrong with spending too much money—money you haven't got. Unfortunately, an overdose of "retail therapy" almost inevitably leads to debt. Shopping is an essential part of life but not when it involves buying things we think we want, rather than the things we actually need. Enjoyable shopping shouldn't end in tears, so if you're prone to buy wildly, just because you need that feel-good lift, do the necessary budget exercise before you set off for the stores.

Figure out which things on your list are essential, which are medium priority, and which low priority. You'll usually find there's a little of each, but focus on the essentials and, above all, use the list. You really have to do this if you're going to stay in control of your finances and not let them control you. It's those wild, impulsive buys that really do the damage. They weren't even on the low priority list, so how can they be justified? Impulse buying is all about losing control. And it's almost certainly going to lead to debts.

Hey, big spender!

Elton John, the British music star, is a star of retail therapy, too. He loves clothes and cars and art and—well, he just loves spending his money. And why not? John's private fortune allows him to pay out $446,000 in credit card bills each month. But that's nothing compared to the $523,000 he spent on flowers between January 1996 and September 1997. In all, it was estimated he spent $2.7 million per month and $17 million on property. He is still said to be worth more than $285 million – and still spending.

Peer pressure

There's nothing easy about resisting peer pressure. The need to fit in stays with us for most of our lives, and copying classmates and friends, aspiring to magazine pictures of the trendy, judging yourself by what others say about you is all part of this pattern. You have to be pretty gutsy to stand out from the crowd and do your own thing. But doing what is best for YOU, wearing what suits YOU, and expressing your own opinions is part of being YOU and not a copycat of everybody else. Remember that manufacturers, retailers, and advertisers worldwide are relying on you to do what everybody else does. They make money by creating mass fashions, mass attitudes, and mass buying fads. Being one of the crowd is comfortable—but don't let your peers influence you too much. There's a subtle kind of pressure that comes close to bullying and obliges people to conform or be considered odd, to spend or risk being labeled shabby. Rise above it all!

Shopaholic

For some people, shopping is the medicine for a far more serious need—these people feel so badly about themselves that shopping becomes a compulsion. It becomes an escape from all of their problems and a driving force in their lives. For these people, shopping is an illness, and the thing that drives them to shop is often their increasing debt.

If you get into the shopping habit and feel that things are getting out of control, there are people who will help you in confidence. Your parents or an older friend can help, too. But do get help. The need to buy, mostly things you don't even want and cannot use, is not just a phase. It is a real illness and needs help and sympathetic treatment.

Conspicuous consumption

The woman or man with a Rolls Royce almost certainly likes the car because it's a great drive, it has good leg room, it's comfortable, and it has roomy trunk space. Then again, they may be the victims of conspicuous consumption. If they have three or four Rolls Royces, they almost certainly are!

If you spend your money on things that everyone recognizes are expensive, if you buy things simply to put out the message that you're wealthy, then this is a label that may well be attached to you one day.

Instant Gratification

You have money to spend and it's burning a hole in your pocket. You march into the store and order the biggest and best music system that's going. But it's out of stock. You've got to wait three weeks for the next one to be delivered. And you're livid!

You want to buy a new outfit but you're short of the last few dollars. Your parents flatly refuse to lend you the money and advise you to wait until you've saved up. You're livid!

Instant gratification is something many young people are increasingly prone to. They want it and they want it NOW. Interestingly, the ability to delay gratification is a sign of superior intelligence!

James Gordon Bennett Jr.

How about this for a big spender? James Gordon Bennett Jr., who was born in 1841, was earning more than $1 million a year by age 25. That's multimillions at present rates! He paid $2 million for a yacht that had a specially designed room to accommodate a cow that supplied fresh milk. He once tipped a porter $14,000, and he bought a restaurant in Monte Carlo on the spot because he arrived for dinner to find someone else sitting at his favorite table. He got the person removed, sat down at his table and ate, and then gave the restaurant deed to one of the waiters as he left.

This extraordinary spender is also remembered as the man who commissioned Henry Morton Stanley to find David Livingstone. Stanley's the one who famously said in 1871, "Doctor Livingstone, I presume," to the British explorer everyone thought was lost in Africa.

Price is right

Thousands of years ago, when people finally had time to grow or make more things than they needed, they might have had a spare cow or a few pairs of furry leggings that they wanted to get rid of. But what would they charge for these items? What would be a fair price? It might have been a couple of goats for the cow or a neat head warmer for the leggings. All well and good. But what if no one needed a cow? You might have to accept just one goat to get rid of it. Or what if everybody wanted one? You might be able to get three or even four goats for it.

The price you ask for something often depends on who wants it—the market. Sellers talk about market forces determining prices. They just mean whether anyone wants the product or not.

Nothing has changed since our ancestors first put a price on their cow. Price also depends on need. We need food, so we are willing to pay for it. If an item becomes scarce, its price will go up because people are willing to pay more just to get it. If there's too much of a thing, the price will come down. Of course, there are other factors that determine the price tag, such as taxes, discounting, and so on.

PRICING THE GOODS

The manufacturer adds up the cost of the materials, the labor, and all the other costs. A profit of 20 percent is added to the total.	The wholesaler adds up the cost of moving the goods to the warehouse, getting orders, and packing and sending to retailers. A profit of 20 percent is added to the total.	The retailer adds up the cost of display, advertising, selling, and other basic costs. A profit of 60 percent is added to the total.	The customer buys the product at the marked-up price.
Original cost = 50 cents ADDS Profit = 10 cents Sells at 60 cents	Buys at 60 cents ADDS Costs = 20 cents Profit = 16 cents Cost price = 96 cents	Buys at 96 cents ADDS Costs = 50 cents Profit = 88 cents Cost price = $2.34	Final selling price = $2.34

Figuring it out

In order to sell an item of goods, the seller has to manufacture it or buy it from someone else or a distributor. The price they pay is called the cost price. It's from this that the final, or retail price, is worked out.

Margin

The difference between what the seller pays for an item and then spends in costs and what the item sells for is called the margin. The seller's costs will be things like storage, distribution, wages, rent, and any taxes. The profit margin is added to arrive at the sales, or retail, price. Some industries calculate a selling price as five times cost price.

Price wars

Price wars are good for the consumer—that's you and me—but not so good for the retailer. They start when one company lowers its price to attract more customers. This often happens at gas stations. The station down the road sees the new price and lowers theirs. Soon everyone is doing the same thing. The gas stations become trapped in a price war. Of course, if they lower prices so that they no longer make a profit, prices start to rise again.

Cargo to warehouse

If goods are to be exported, or sold outside their home country, they have to be shipped in some kind of way. Food might have to travel in refrigerated trucks, while cars might need to be chained in special holds on ships so they won't roll around during the voyage. Other goods are shipped in large containers that can be loaded onto trucks, taken to a dock or airport, and loaded intact onto a ship or plane.

There's lots of documentation that accompanies these goods. One document is the waybill or airwaybill. The carrier of the goods prepares the waybill by giving a description of the goods and the name of the buyer and seller. Then there'll be customs forms and the all-important proof of sale—the bill of exchange.

In today's high-tech world of international trade, most transactions are carried out over the phone, over the Internet, or with a bill of exchange. If a bill of exchange is used, one trader decides what amount must be sent to another trader, then orders their bank to pay it. The bill of exchange shows the amount required, the currency in which it is to be paid, and the date by which it has to be paid. Once they've landed at the dock or airport, the goods are taken to a warehouse and stored until they've passed customs inspection.

Warehouse to counter

Once goods have been OK'd by customs they are ready to be moved from the warehouse to the counter of your local store. The movement of goods is called the distribution system.

Sometimes a company has its own distribution arm, with trucks or rail links, but many use specialized distribution companies. From the warehouse, goods may be moved to the warehouses of the company, or they may go to a middleman called a wholesaler.

Wholesalers can store a great many different things, so sometimes it's more convenient for retailers to buy from them. Finally, either from a wholesaler, the store's warehouse, or straight from the docks, the goods reach the counter and can be sold to you and me—the consumer. The price we pay has to take into account all of the different steps taken to get the goods to us, plus the profit the store wants to make.

The sales

Twice a year—and even more often—stores change their stock. Summer clothes give way to winter clothes, old stock gets replaced by new models, items that haven't sold get reduced to make more space in the warehouse. It's sales time.

What is likely to happen to prices? The retailers aren't going to lose money if they can help it, so don't expect big reductions at first. What you will find is something in this season's color that's going cheap because it is going out of favor. This year's model is worthless in the fashion-crazed world of electronics—so again, expect real bargains.

Spotting a bargain

There are always a few real bargains in a sale—and a lot that isn't. After all, sales are all about getting rid of unsold stock, so you're unlikely to find the top fashion item of the season sitting with a 25 percent off label. But you might well find the article you wanted the week before but were sensible enough not to buy until the sales started. If you've held back, if you know exactly what you want, if you've spotted it in the window and know you'll get it marked down, then start lining up! Know what you want and be first in line to get it!

Loot in the attic

Have you watched those TV programs where people line up to show the experts what they've hidden in a rumpled brown bag—a family treasure that's been sitting in the attic since grandma put it there 50 years ago? And lo and behold, it's got a mark on the back that shows it was made by a famous silversmith or painter or potter—and it's worth $1,000! Well it's time to get up in the attic and look around. How do you know how to pick out a decent item from among the junk? Well, there are lots of practical guides, both in book form and via Web sites, that explain how to spot a treasure and how to sell it.

10 percent discount!

It's a sad fact that many retailers know that people are looking for bargains at sale time, so they make sure they have some by buying goods especially for the sale. The stores get flooded with cheap manufactured items that cost practically nothing to make and practically nothing to buy.

Look for a label that guarantees the store quality. Often, these goods come in under a different brand—their job is to act as magnets to get people into the store. You've seen piles of boxes, racks of clothes,

mounds of teddy bears, near the door or in the window— irresistibly close!

Remember!

You can lose certain rights as a consumer when you buy goods in the sales. Many stores state clearly that sale goods cannot be returned for any reason.

Buying off the Web

In 2001, a data monitoring company predicted that teenagers in the U.S. and Europe would spend $10.6 billion online by 2005. They went on to suggest that teenage online spending would be driven by the availability of prepaid cards, and that merchants would have to integrate new payment systems if they wanted to target this market. Well, it didn't take long before payment systems were found, and the teen market opened for practically unlimited business. And, of course, they didn't anticipate the success of eBay!

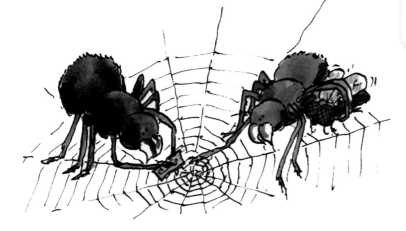

Bigger spenders

Marketing people are happy to urge young people to buy for fun and satisfaction. And the trend now is for more and more spending to be done when the urge takes you—online. According to some reports, teen spending will soon outstrip adult spending online. Studies also showed that in 2002 males were spending an average of $70 per week online and females $64 per week online. That's a lot. But then, when you can use a credit card online 24 hours a day, seven days a week, it's easy.

eBay

A guy called Pierre Omidyar set up eBay in 1995 so he could sell something. Since then it has grown and grown, and today it's the largest online auction market in the world. Imagine more than 100 million people all buying and selling to each other! It is just like a local street market, but in cyberspace. People not only buy and sell on this global auction site, but they chat and argue, too, just like they did in the old marketplaces of hundreds of years ago.

A recent survey showed that 724,000 Americans saw eBay as their primary or secondary source of income. As well as professional eBay sellers, another 1.5 million people said that they added to their income by selling stuff on eBay.

You have to be 18 to register as a seller, since you'd be entering into a legal contract with someone around the world. However, as with many accounts and investments, you can go into partnership with a parent who will take responsibility for the account registration.

Talk the Biz!

Comparison shopping

One way to make sure you get value for your money is to do what's known as comparison shopping. Prices are compared in a number of outlets and sometimes published in consumer magazines.

Profiteering

Everyone understands that a company must make a profit, but sometimes profits are spiked up when a product is scarce or when there's a great need for it. This is called profiteering, and it's not ethical.

Buying on credit

American teens spend an estimated $150 billion every year on consumer goods, and that makes them a prime target for credit card companies looking to be the first to put plastic in their eager hands. But if young people aren't properly prepared to spend responsibly, they could be heading for years of financial difficulty. Despite teen spending power, parents are often reluctant to entrust their children with the responsibility of a typical debit or credit card. They know all too well what credit card debt can lead to.

However, while previous generations tended to save their money before buying, many young people will choose to purchase goods on credit. Sound financial education can play an important part in helping them understand credit arrangements and manage debt.

Some parents are happy to introduce their teens to credit cards on the basis that there's a degree of control at this stage, and that education is better than ignorance.

• How much money do you have each month after subtracting monthly expenses?
• What should a credit card be used for—emergencies and parent-authorized purchases?
• How will you and your parents keep track of your credit spending—dual copies of bills and credit statements?

Get these questions sorted so you can set up your credit card spending on the right footing and know you will gain valuable financial experience before you leave home.

Credit card king!

Walter Cavanagh of Santa Clara, California, has a record 1,397 separate credit cards. If he wants to go shopping, his cards allow him to spend a cool $1.6 million!

No!
Don't try it!

Receipt

Always keep your receipt. This is a document that a seller, merchant, or vendor hands to a customer acknowledging that they have received an amount of money in exchange for an item or service. Usually a receipt is given at the end of an exchange if the vendor has been paid in cash, or when the customer asks for it. Sometimes making out a receipt is required by law. If you pay by credit card, the documentation produced by the card machine is enough to act as a receipt.

Because a receipt is a proof of purchase, it's wise to hang on to it. It may be needed if you want to exchange what you've bought for something else. And always check receipts, especially in restaurants. Make sure what's on there is what you actually bought and that there are no hidden costs you didn't know about.

A card of your own

Some young people carry a "teen card," which is a prepaid stored value card. The card program is aimed at the under-20 market. Parents load the card with credit to an agreed level. Such reloadable cards can be a valuable tool to help young consumers learn fiscal responsibility, while developing a lasting relationship with a financial institution.

Consumer rights

Consumer law

1. Packaging and labeling

The law says that all labels on products must give accurate information about the size, price, and ingredients of that product. If the box is larger than the product and might give a false impression of its size, you are supposed to declare this, too.

2. Danger!

Products that are poisonous, sharp, or dangerous in any way, must carry a warning on the outside. This can be as simple as a caution label. It is important to do this for products used by very young children and old people especially.

3. Origin

In many countries it is necessary to state on the labeling where a product has been made or manufactured.

4. Prices

All products sold in stores must carry a price label, which is the price to be paid. Price labels don't have taxes added, so somewhere customers have to be told this, too.

5. Trademarks

A product or brand name can be legally protected from any people who want to copy it, by giving it a trademark. This goes for store names, too.

6. Warranty

Most products carry a full warranty. This is a promise by the manufacturer, and sometimes the retailer, that if a product has a fault or goes wrong, it will be fixed or replaced at no cost to you. A limited warranty means that only certain parts of the product are covered. Remember to complete the warranty slip that comes with your purchase and send it off as required.

Even if there's no written warranty agreement, the law states that all manufacturers must guarantee that their products do what they are supposed to do. If they don't, you can demand your money back or a replacement.

We often read that we live in a consumer society—and we do. But who are these consumers that make up the society? Well, they're you and me and everyone else that buys things and uses the services that other people provide. It's our ability and need to consume that keeps the world turning today. We are no longer a society that works mostly at producing its own food and clothing and other essentials. We work at other things to earn money to get those essentials. But at the same time, we need to buy what people sell and use the services they provide in order for them to earn money. It kind of moves in a circle. Of course, we consumers can only buy what suppliers make available to us—and that sort of puts them in the driver's seat. But we consumers do have some rights, and it's important that we know about them.

Customer complaints

In most places, you may return a product to the store where you bought it for a refund or exchange as long as you do so within a set number of days, usually 28 or so, of purchase. You don't have to give a reason, although you've probably decided it's not working properly, it doesn't fit, it's the wrong color, or you just don't like it.

Remember that you must return the product, in its box or packaging, with the sales tags and the receipt you were handed at the till. Salespeople are trained to accept returned goods, so don't feel intimidated or shy. Be courteous and open and you should get a refund, an exchange, or a credit to spend at the store. However, if you don't get treated fairly or think the store or service provider is doing something it shouldn't, there are regulatory bodies you can complain to.

What a waste!

How many pairs of jeans have you got in your closet? How many T-shirts, blouses, or other unworn clothes are there that have never been taken off the hanger? We buy for all kinds of reasons, but rarely because we don't have something. It's more likely to be for a quite different reason—and not one that makes a lot of sense!

Too much choice

If you want a chocolate bar, you have 20 to choose from. Need a breakfast cereal? There are 50 kinds! A sweater—100! When it comes to food and clothing, we're spoiled for choice. There was a time when things like these were essentials. In fact, during World War II you had to take your ration book to the store to get your permitted items. This was back in the 1940s, so someone in your family may remember it. It's not that long ago! But today, with goods pouring in from all over the world, there's more than enough for everyone—and no one has to line up for a pair of winter boots.

In many developed countries, people have become such expert consumers that they overbuy knowingly. And many throw away a large proportion of what they buy and think nothing of it. In the United Kingdom, it's been calculated that people throw away nearly 40 percent of the food they buy. We throw out clothes because they look a bit dated or worn at the edges. Maybe the fashion has changed or we just never liked them in the first place. The truth is, we've become very wasteful.

New and cheap

Compared to the old days of rationing, there's no doubt that we've become spoiled. We're almost all shopaholics, albeit in a mild form. We're wasteful, throwing things away because they're not new. New is everything. We like the latest product even if the one we have is only a few months old. We throw food away, not because it's gone bad, but because we have a crisper, fresher version. We throw a shirt away because it would cost more to take it to the cleaners than to replace it.

Play shopping!

Did you ever play store when you were young? You were probably quite serious about setting out your wares and counting out the change. And what really gave you a thrill was filling the till with coins. Today, with shopping malls that entertain us, feed us, play us music, and generally offer us everything we need for a good day out, it's impossible to see shopping as anything else but recreation. It's our number one hobby. It's a place for meeting friends and socializing.

Land-fillers

But the more we shop, the more we waste. Tons and tons of things we've bought are dumped in waste baskets by each family, each year. It costs billions to deal with it and much of it does nothing to help the environment. There are famous pictures of planet Earth drowning in its own junk! And while we're ruining our planet and filling every crack we have with our garbage, we're also doing nothing to help those who don't enjoy our prosperity.

Ethics

When we think of the ethics of buying and selling we usually think of stuff like animal testing. We don't believe it's ethical, or morally right, to test the products we buy on animals. So many manufacturers state that their products are not tested on animals. But ethics covers more than just animal testing. It may concern the people who grow or make certain items or the way stuff is advertised or even what substances are put into food.

We all know that fast food can be bad for us, but we still consume lots of it. Fast food companies have for years been targeting young people and showing their foods as the only really "cool" thing to eat. Fats and sugars are used to make the stuff taste good. So is it ethical to sell in this way? Some people think not, and fast food chains are beginning to change their menus to include more healthy items.

Recycle it!

Here are some basic questions about the environment and recycling. How much do you know?

1. Which of the following are generally recyclable?
A. Aluminum
B. Glass
C. Paper
D. Plastic
E. Tin
F. All of the above
G. None of the above

2. Which could you find another use for before you recycle it?
A. Glass jar
B. Paper only used on one side
C. Plastic milk jug or soda bottle
D. Tin can
E. All of the above
F. None of the above

3. Which of these are benefits to recycling?
A. Conserves energy
B. Conserves resources
C. Conserves landfill space
D. Prevents litter
E. Makes you feel good
F. All of the above
G. None of the above

4. Which is the most difficult to recycle?
A. Glass
B. Paper
C. Plastic
D. Tin cans
E. Aluminum

5. Can you recycle paper?
A. Yes   B. No

6. What product can pollute 250,000 times more than it weighs?
A. Plastic
B. Batteries
C. Oil
D. Paper
E. Tires

7. Which would be the best store bag to use?
A. A brown paper bag
B. A plastic bag
C. A cloth bag
D. A recycled cloth bag
E. All of the above
F. None of the above

ANSWERS on page 45

Green buying

Are you a "conscious" shopper? Are you purchasing school notebooks created from recycled paper and buying organic chocolate? If you are, you've been won over to "green shopping." This also involves buying from people who have been paid a fair amount for what they've produced, whether it's coffee or handbags, and buying from people whose working conditions are good. Some stores are dedicated to selling items that don't include animal testing and that are bought for a fair price—often from what we call the third world.

In a way, green buying takes us back to ethics. It's about purchasing stuff that's healthy or that doesn't hurt the environment. Working together with millions of others, every one of us can help change the world; and it isn't that hard. Just changing the things you buy a little bit, when added to the actions of many others, can have a huge impact. All of this buying is affecting the world we live in. The fact is that our buy-and-throw-away culture is taking a heavy toll on the world. Although we don't always see the effects, all that we buy comes from the earth and returns to it in one form or another.

The good thing is that you're the one in charge. Green buying isn't always easy because you may have to pay a bit more for your items and because outlets are hard to find. But it's worth it in the end. Remember—buy stuff that's better for the planet and you'll make a difference.

Selling: So can you sell?

Most people are pretty good at buying. They feel comfortable with money in their wallet and a shopping list in their hand. They enjoy the excitement of choosing new things and swinging out of the store with a crisp new shopping bag. But very few feel as comfortable about selling.

For some reason, few people enjoy being on the other side of the counter nearly as much. But selling can be far more satisfying. Telling people about your service or your product, getting them to buy, and finally, pocketing the cash you have made, can be very rewarding!

Just imagine: Your team has just won the semifinals and you've got to the finals for the first time. Some of your teammates are a bit overwhelmed by it all, but not you. You can't wait to get to the last game and win it. That's because you're competitive. And if you're competitive, you might just make a good salesperson.

On the other hand, you may have set up a business buying cakes for very little and selling them at a generous profit. It's not so much the money you earn that makes it fun, it's the deal you did to get the stuff so cheaply. You love doing deals. Well, there's a good chance you'll make a good salesperson, too.

Can you sell?

In fact, we're all salespeople at heart. Persuading your friends that your argument is the right one often takes a bit of a sales job. Convincing your parents that you should receive a weekly allowance for keeping your room tidy could be even tougher! Selling is the same whether you're persuading people to buy into your ideas, your cooperation or your products. And we do it all the time!

However, for those for whom selling doesn't come easily, these are the six easy steps to use:

1. Identify YOUR goals. You want to get rid of something; you want to make money selling it; you need the money to buy something you want; you want to earn money to prove you can.

2. Expect a YES. If you approach your customer expecting them to say NO, they almost certainly will. Why? Because people respond best to a positive, confident approach. If you look as if you have something worthwhile to sell, your customer will pick up on that and you'll get their attention.

3. Smile! Be friendly and good-mannered. This is a must for a salesperson.

4. Explain the good points about what you are selling. Practice this well in advance and get your facts word-perfect. Keep it short and to the point. People have an amazingly short attention span!

5. Ask your customer to buy. Don't beat around the bush. The trick is to ask a question that doesn't need the reply yes or no. Don't try "Would you like to buy one?" Your question needs an answer that is "Yes, NOW!" Try an approach like "Would you like the large one or the small one?" You are assuming they will buy immediately, and the only question to be decided is what size.

6. If you get an answer of no, don't give up. Find another potential customer at once—you mustn't lose heart—and start all over again.

The entertainers

In a sense, salespeople, like advertising people, are entertainers. They need to get your attention quickly and point out all the good things about their product without boring you stiff. They can do this by making you laugh, telling a good story, or capturing your imagination.

Marketing people know all the emotional tricks. They know how to make you feel good about the product. Just look at the next car ad you see on TV. What does it say about the car? Probably not very much. But it does say a lot about the lifestyle you'll achieve if you buy it. It might also suggest that it'll bring you the boyfriend or girlfriend of your dreams!

This is clever selling, but we, the buyer, have to beware. We have to know that a new razor is not going to make us into a basketball superstar or that a new hair shade won't nab us a rich boyfriend. More importantly, we have to know that supposed medical-based claims, such as "antiwrinkle creams will make you look younger," are myths. They don't work! So for all the clever sales stuff we see, we have to apply our buyer brains. As a consumer, you should be told the truth about a product. If you aren't, there are watchdogs to help you.

Selling your stuff

For every person who buys, there is someone who sells. For every item you buy, there's probably one you want to dump. How can you sell your stuff and get the best price for it?

Your best customers are likely to be people your age with shared tastes, so set up a collective sale with a group of friends. You'll need a venue and a set day and you'll need to advertise the event well. This won't be difficult if you're still in school. Why not offer a percentage of the money you all make to a charity? You'll get more support this way, and you'll be doing something worthwhile. Make sure you post the results of your donation so everyone knows you did what you promised—and they can feel good, too.

There may be local junk or secondhand shops that aren't charity shops, but outlets where you may get a penny or two for your secondhand possessions. There's nothing to stop you from organizing your own garage or yard sale. Again, get friends and family involved and make a professional event out of it.

If you think you've got something of value, try selling it on eBay. Or if you're going to make a business out of this, selling a service or a product all your own, then take the real entrepreneurial route, and set up your own Web site to advertise your wares.

Only 2 to 3 percent of actual sales come from cold calling, but sales people are getting their name out, and next time—who knows!

International trade

Thousands of years ago, when people first settled into villages and started farming, they got rid of their extra products by trading with other villages. At the same time, some villages became better at doing certain things than others—making arrowheads or woolly mammoth pendants. This is called specialization and it created an even wider demand for trade.

Today, the same thing applies on a far bigger scale. Countries tend to concentrate on producing goods and services where they have a natural advantage over other countries. A nation such as Canada, for instance, produces a lot of wheat because it has wide areas of plains land that make wheat growing possible. Saudi Arabia produces mainly oil because it has huge natural oil deposits. In each case, a proportion of the output can be exchanged, or traded, for other goods, just like trade between the ancient villages. This is called international trade.

Coins like the euro, Swiss franc, and Australian dollar are some of hundreds of different world currencies.

The money problem

One of the big differences between domestic trade, or trade within a country, and international trade, is that with international trade different currencies may have to be used. So before international trading can take place, it has to be possible to trade currencies. For instance, if you wanted to buy lanterns from China, you'd have to pay in Chinese yuan. This means you'd have to be able to buy yuan with your dollars, pounds, or pesos. Sometimes

trade is made easier when traders agree to work in one currency, such as the dollar. Still, international traders have to be aware of the price of buying foreign currency and how it will affect the cost of the goods they are buying.

Let's say there were only two countries, Saudi Arabia and Jamaica. Saudi Arabia produces more oil than it can possibly use. But it can't grow sugar cane, and everyone wants sugar. Jamaica can grow loads of sugar cane because it has the right climate, but it needs oil for gas, heating fuel, and so on. Providing there are no barriers to trading, Saudi Arabia can trade oil to Jamaica, while Jamaica can trade sugar to Saudi Arabia. This kind of specialization in trade allows countries to sell goods and earn money to buy materials they may not be able to produce themselves.

Helping out:

Tariffs

Governments also make money from international trade. They do this by imposing duty, called a tariff or customs tax, on goods that enter their country. Customs officers are employed to check goods coming in and apply the correct tariff.

There are two main types of tariffs. Specific tariffs are where a quantity of an item, such as a barrel of oil, is taxed regardless of its value. An "ad valorem" tariff applies when a tax is calculated as a percentage of the price.

Believe it or not, taxes can also be used as a kind of weapon against another country. If country A wants to damage country B for some injustice it considers has been done, it can apply such huge tariffs that country B can't sell its goods into country A. Of course, country B might then retaliate by using the same weapon—and a so-called trade war begins.

Trade department

Like most things, international trade needs certain rules and regulations in order to run smoothly. In most countries a government body called the Board of Trade, Trade Department, or some similar name is set up. Its work is to supervise and control the regulations that govern trading, both domestic and international.

The department also helps to promote international trade. It may also offer some kinds of aid through a credit agency. To help other countries know what its own country has to offer, it might also set up trade fairs where companies can show off their goods to foreign buyers.

Chamber of commerce

A chamber of commerce makes international trade easier to carry out. It is an organization that represents all of the various branches of trade and industry, such as manufacturers, distributors, or anyone else who is part of the business community. Its job is to help its members find business opportunities at home and abroad and to make sure they know the laws and regulations of the countries they're trading with. It collects and distributes information and makes presentations to the governments when new laws that might affect its members are proposed.

Fair Trade

A lot has been said about the way some large corporations bully suppliers in poor countries into selling their goods at low prices. The corporations are able to make very large profits for themselves, but the suppliers are left to live lives of poverty and hardship. Large corporations can get away with this because their wealth gives them great power—enough to sway governments. Of course, this isn't fair. So some smaller companies have helped to set up systems called fair trade, where the farmer or other supplier is paid a fair amount for the goods they supply. The Fair Trade Coffee Company, for instance, makes sure its coffee farmers aren't underpaid. Their coffee is sold in many stores.

Balance of trade

Sometimes you hear a TV reporter telling you that the trade balance of your country is "up or down" or "It's the worst it's ever been under this government." The figures they give out are in millions of dollars, or even billions. You may well scratch your head and wonder what you've been missing, who's doing all this trading, and why so much money is involved? Well, it's less complicated than you might think.

A country's trade balance is about what the country has sold abroad and what it has bought from abroad. This is international trade. It's as if the country itself were a large store that sells to other stores, that are other countries. America Inc. sells to England Inc., China Co., Brazil Ltd., and so on. China Co. sells to England Inc., America Inc., and whoever else wants its products. The difference between what a country sells and what it buys is the trade gap, and the two figures make up the trade balance.

Imports

Goods and services that are brought into a country to sell are called imports. The imports cost nations money because the company that imports them has to pay for them. So money moves out of the country. Countries import goods or services because they cannot produce them for themselves and they're necessary, or because they're cheaper to buy abroad than to manufacture at home. Most imports have some restrictions applied to them, such as an import tax, known as duty.

Often, only a certain amount of an item can be brought into a country. This is called a quota. Let's say lots of workers in your country earn their living by making cars. If too many cheaper, foreign cars were allowed in, fewer local cars might be bought and workers would lose their jobs. This kind of protection is sometimes necessary.

Balance or gap?

It would be great if a country sold more than it bought from abroad. That would mean the trade balance was in its favor. The country would be making money. But that can't always happen. Some countries have to buy in more than they sell. This creates a negative trade balance and the country is spending more than it's earning, leaving a huge gap.

Sometimes, of course, the figures even out so there's an overall trade balance with no gap at all. That's the ideal situation.

A positive balance of trade is especially good. First of all, the people who manufacture products or offer services make more money than they would if they just sold in their own country. Secondly, the government makes money by charging taxes on everything that comes into the country.

Exports

Exports are goods and services that are supplied to and bought by companies or governments in other countries. Exporting, or selling lots of goods abroad, is good for a country because it brings cash in and creates wealth. Money earned from exports benefits a country's balance of payments.

Exports are usually paid for in the currency of the supplier. They may be goods and services that a country can produce easily or that are wanted by countries abroad. America exports athletic shoes because they're popular, not because countries need them. However, America has large areas of land that are just right for wheat growing. So it exports wheat to countries that cannot grow wheat for themselves.

The economy

The economy of a country is the way in which it deals with its resources and the demands or needs of its people. The economy depends on the state of a country at any one time. For instance, if a country is at war it will demand huge amounts of military equipment so more resources, including the people, will have to be employed in making it. Fewer resources will be used to make luxury goods. A country that has large resources of gold and silver and is relatively rich and peaceful, on the other hand, can use more resources to make luxury goods and other nonessential things.

Market economy

Countries like the United States, Great Britain, and Japan have what is called a market economy. This means decisions about production and the allocation of resources are left to private individuals, companies, and corporations. It's part of the idea of democracy. The private individuals work through a price system. In other words, companies will charge prices that people can afford. People will buy goods, earn money, produce more goods, and so on. Rewards are based on individual efforts, and wealth is produced through trade.

Planned economy

In a planned economy, the government makes decisions about production and allocation of resources. It decides what will be produced and how much it will cost. In theory, planned economies should make things available for everyone to buy, and there shouldn't be a huge gap between rich and poor. But this rarely happens. Communism is a planned economy that has failed in most cases. Rewards are not necessarily based on individual efforts but on the efforts of the state as a whole.

Surpluses

Sometimes a country produces more of a certain product or food than it can use itself or sell abroad. This is called a surplus. Surpluses can mount up and cause real difficulties. Let's take wheat, for instance. You might think the answer to having too much wheat would be to give it away to starving people in poorer countries. But there's a problem. If you gave the wheat away, no one would want to pay the proper price for it. The price of wheat would drop. Another unpopular solution is to pay farmers not to grow it.

Visible or invisible?

Visible exports

Manufactured goods are the visible part of exports. They can involve every kind of product from steel bridges to matchsticks. You need raw materials and labor to manufacture. Countries with lots of raw materials, such as steel, coal, or wood, are good at manufacturing. Sometimes, however, raw materials run out or become too expensive to get ahold of, and manufacturing has to slow down.

Invisible exports

Selling services is known as the invisible part of exports. Services include things such as banking, insurance, car rental, catering, computer servicing, and so on. These industries don't actually manufacture anything themselves, but they help other people or companies to do so.

Spending abroad

Everyone loves vacations, whether it's summer or winter. If you're going somewhere new and exciting, it's something you look forward to. You buy what you need for the trip, perhaps a new swimsuit, snorkel, a pair of walking shoes, or a new ski hat. You get the tickets, and you're ready to go ... except for one thing. The country you're going to uses a funny kind of money you've never heard of. And you've read that if you want to buy something you might have to haggle over the price, something you wouldn't dream of doing at your local stores. But fear not. Once you've learned the ins and outs of spending abroad you'll have no trouble at all.

Is it a bargain?

You've just seen the coolest leather jacket ever made, and you want it badly. And what's even better, it doesn't seem overly expensive. In fact, it's just within your budget. You pick it up, take it to the counter, and tell the salesperson you want it. She tells you the price, and you nearly pass out. But it's not the price on the jacket at all. You point to the ticket, your mouth open, and the salesperson smiles. "That's without the sales tax," she says.

Disappointed, you put the jacket back and walk out of the store. With the sales tax added it's well above your budget.

The moral of this story is that what looks like a bargain at first glance may not be one at all. Many countries impose sales tax, but stores don't show it on the price tag. This is done for obvious reasons. If you live in the country, you automatically add on the tax amount. But if you don't, you might be persuaded to buy something you want out of embarrassment or because you just can't part with it. Always find out if a country or state imposes sales tax. This can differ within countries, so always ask if you're not sure.

In many countries haggling is part of the fun of buying. It might take some getting used to, but shopkeepers expect it, so don't be shy. Get the lowest price you can. But beware of badly made items. Often, if an item sells for a ridiculously low price, it probably cost even less to make, so it may not be of the highest quality. You get what you pay for!

What's good where?

Italy
Leather goods, designer clothes, including all the big names in Milan and Rome

North Africa
Items from the souks—leather goods, jewelry, beaten metal objects

France
wines, perfumes, foods, fashion

Spain
Leather goods, including shoes, coats, and bags

Indonesia
Puppets, wood carvings, fabrics, cane and carved wood furniture, jewelry

India
Spices, decorations, ornamental brass plates, richly colored silks and fabrics

Foreign exchange

The first step to buying things abroad is to get hold of some of the money you've never heard of. It would be much easier if every country in the world had developed the same kind of money—we'd all be using a "worldthalar" and cents or a "credit," as the early sci-fi writers called it. You wouldn't have to go to a money changer or to the currency exchange counter in a bank (and pay a fee) whenever you wanted to travel and needed foreign currency.

But if you're going on a vacation to a foreign country you'll need to buy foreign currency. For instance, if you're going to France you'll need euros, if you're going to the United Kingdom you'll need pounds, and if you're going to China you'll need yuan. You can buy foreign currency at a bank or at an agency such as American Express.

Each seller will charge a fee for making the exchange, which might be a small percentage of

the total with a minimum amount per transaction. Watch for exchange rates used, because now that currencies "float," different companies can use higher or lower rates. You might, for instance, get a better rate of exchange at a bank or online than at an agency. Be aware as well that exchange rates are different when you buy compared to when you sell. You'll always get a better rate when you buy. Money changers usually give both rates. So it's best to get rid of all your foreign money before you return home.

Bringing it home

When you bring home your precious holiday keepsakes and gifts, you'll have to bring them through customs. Customs officers may check your luggage to make sure there's nothing hidden in it that you don't want them to see. And we don't mean the silly hat you bought on the beach. We mean any stuff that you might have to pay customs duty, or tax, on. You may have to pay tax on

excess items or cameras and watches. Make sure you know what your tax allowances are. The flight attendants on the plane can help. But it's best if you check at the store when you're buying an item, if it's possible. You don't want to have anything taken away from you, so be sure you have money to pay the duty if you have to. And declare what you have to pay duty on. Not declaring it is an offense.

Different habits

One thing you must remember when visiting another country and going into any public building, including stores, is that different countries have different customs.

For instance, in Bahrain you would not sit with the soles of your shoes showing, since this is an insulting gesture. In Brazil you should not make the OK sign with forefinger and thumb—very insulting. In Arabic-speaking countries when you're haggling over prices, be firm but polite, and bear in mind that time does not have quite the same significance it has to foreigners. In Japan return a short bow and always be polite.

Glossary

auction
An auction is a form of public sale where goods are offered for sale without a given price. Each is sold to the person who offers the most.

bid
A bid is an offer of money to buy an item on sale at an auction.

bill of exchange
A bill of exchange is a document confirming that goods bought overseas have been paid for according to the information given.

boutique
A boutique is a small shop that specializes in selling one or just a few kinds of products.

brand
A brand is the recognizable trademark and logo used to identify an item or set of goods, and which is used to advertise and sell them.

budget
A budget is an estimate of money expected to be paid or received in the future.

charity
A charity is an organization set up to help those people who cannot afford, or who cannot get, the help they need.

check
A check is a printed piece of paper that orders a bank to pay money out of a customer's account.

consumer
A consumer is another name for a person who is a regular purchaser of household and other goods.

credit
Credit is an arrangement a customer makes to pay for goods at a later date.

credit card
A credit card is a plastic card used to buy goods and services to be paid for at a later date.

currency
Currency is the money used by a particular country.

customs
Customs is a department of the government that monitors and collects duties and taxes on goods entering the country.

debit card
A debit card is a plastic card that is used like a check to pay for goods. It promises to pay for the goods out of the holder's bank account.

debt
A debt is an amount of money that is owed to someone.

demographics
Demographics describes the process of counting people and tracking and recording their living habits.

direct mail
Direct mail is a method of advertising, selling, and distributing goods, using catalogs, advertisements in magazines, flyers, and the Internet to find customers. Deliveries are made using the postal system.

discount
A discount is a reduction in price.

duty
Duty is a tax placed on goods entering a country.

economy
The economy of a country is everything to do with the way it produces things and sells them.

environment
An environment is another name for surroundings that have special conditions and characteristics.

ethics
Ethics are a code of behavior that set out how people should behave in a fair and proper manner.

export
To export is to sell goods or services overseas.

gamble
To gamble means to take a risk to make money.

haberdasher

Haberdasher is the old-fashioned name given to a seller of dressmaking and sewing goods.

haggle
To haggle is to argue about the price of something. The purpose of haggling is to reach a price on which both buyer and seller agree.

international trade
International trade is the name given to all buying and selling between the countries of the world.

invest
To invest means to spend money in order to earn more money.

logo
A logo is a design used to identify an item or set of goods. Logos are used in packaging and advertising the goods.

mail order
Mail order is a method of purchasing and distributing goods. They are bought from catalogs and from ads placed in newspapers and other publications and delivered by mail.

margin
Margin is another name for profit. It is the sum of money left over when all the costs have been deducted from the selling price.

market
A market is a site where goods are set out for sale. It can also describe a group of buyers.

market research
Market research is information collected from consumers about their purchasing habits.

mark-up
Mark-up describes the number of times the cost of an item is multiplied to reach its selling price.

mint
A mint is a place where coins are manufactured.

peddler
A peddler is a salesperson who travels from place to place selling a small amount of stock.

point of purchase (POP)
Point of purchase describes the method and place where goods are displayed in a store to catch the customer's eye.

profit
Profit is the money earned when income is greater than expenditure.

receipt
A receipt is a document provided to someone who has made a purchase by the seller. It shows the date, goods, and price, and any other information required by law.

recycle
To recycle means to reuse. Many forms of packaging, as well as paper and fabric goods, can be used again and again to save money and resources.

refund
A refund is a repayment of money made when goods are returned to the seller.

reserve price
The reserve price is the minimum sum of money that a seller will accept for the sale of goods at auction.

retail

Retail describes the action of selling.

shoplifting

Shoplifting describes the action of stealing goods from a store. The punishment for shoplifting can be severe.

souk

A souk is a covered market found in many towns of the Arab world.

spending power

Spending power describes the wealth of a section of the population.

sponsor

To sponsor means to support someone by giving them money on a regular basis.

street vendor

Street vendors sell their goods from displays set up on the sidewalk or roadside.

supply and demand

Supply and demand describes the way that manufacturers and retailers react to patterns and trends in consumer buying.

target market

A target market is the group of people selected by a company to advertise and sell goods to.

tariff

A tariff is another name for a tax that can be placed on goods that come in from another country.

tax

Tax is the money paid by people and companies to the government to help fund the running of the country.

telemarketing

Telemarketing is the action of phoning people to sell them goods.

till

A till is a machine used for collecting payments and issuing receipts in a store.

trademark

A trademark is a form of legal registration that shows the owner of a brand or item.

trade route

A trade route is a commonly used path of travel used by merchants who move between different points to trade.

TV shopping

TV shopping describes the act of buying from advertisements shown on shopping channels.

warranty

A warranty is a legal guarantee issued by a supplier. A warranty protects the buyer from damaged or faulty goods and often meets a range of other legal requirements.

wholesale

Wholesale describes the process of warehousing goods. This takes place after they have been moved from the factory or plant and before they reach the stores.

window dressing

Window dressing is the art of displaying goods in a store window so they attract buyers to the store.

Want to Learn More?

At the Library

Harman, Hollis Page. *Money Sense for Kids*! 2nd ed. Hauppauge, N.Y.: Barron's, 2004.

Karlitz, Gail. *Growing Money: A Complete Investing Guide for Kids*. New York: Price Stern Sloan, 1999.

Mayr, Diane. *The Everything Kids' Money Book: From Spending to Saving to Investing—Learn All About Money*! Holbrook, Mass.: Adams Media Corp., 2000.

Otfinoski, Steven. *The Kids' Guide to Money: Earning It, Saving It, Spending It, Sharing It*. New York: Scholastic, 1996.

Look for all the books in this series:

Common Cents
The Money in Your Pocket
0-7565-1671-4

Cowries, Coins, Credit
The History of Money
0-7565-1676-5

Get Rich Quick?
Earning Money
0-7565-1674-9

Money: It's Our Job
Money Careers
0-7565-1675-7

Save, Spend, Share
Using Your Money
0-7565-1672-2

What's It All Worth?
The Value of Money
0-7565-1673-0

On the Web

For more information on *using your money*, use FactHound to track down Web sites related to this book.

1. Go to *www.facthound.com*
2. Type in a search word related to this book or this book ID: 0756516722
3. Click on the *Fetch It* button.
Your trusty FactHound will fetch the best Web sites for you!

Answers to quiz on page 33

Question 1	F. All of the above
Question 2	E. All of the above
Question 3	F. All of the above
Question 4	C: Plastic
Question 5	A. Yes
Question 6	C. Oil
Question 7	E. All of the above

Index